Jacques Cousteau

Jennifer Strand

abdopublishing.com

Published by Abdo Zoom™, PO Box 398166, Minneapolis, Minnesota 55439. Copyright © 2017 by Abdo Consulting Group, Inc. International copyrights reserved in all countries. No part of this book may be reproduced in any form without written permission from the publisher. Abdo Zoom™ is a trademark and logo of Abdo Consulting Group, Inc.

Printed in the United States of America, North Mankato, Minnesota
072016
092016

Cover Photo: Bettmann/Corbis
Interior Photos: Bettmann/Corbis, 1; Bettmann/Getty Images, 4; iStockphoto, 5, 7; Alfred Stieglitz/ Library of Congress, 6; E. J. Johnson Photography/iStockphoto, 8–9; Press Association/AP Images, 9; AFP/ Getty Images, 10; Rene Maestri/AP Images, 11; IS/AP Images, 12–13; Kathy Willens/AP Images, 13; AP Images, 14, 16; Sergiy Zavgorodny/Shutterstock Images, 16–17; Pete Cosgrove/AP Images, 18; Fred Tanneau/AFP/Getty Images, 19

Editor: Emily Temple
Series Designer: Madeline Berger
Art Direction: Dorothy Toth

Publisher's Cataloging-in-Publication Data
Names: Strand, Jennifer, author.
Title: Jacques Cousteau / by Jennifer Strand.
Description: Minneapolis, MN : Abdo Zoom, [2017] | Series: Pioneering explorers | Includes bibliographical references and index.
Identifiers: LCCN 2016941516 | ISBN 9781680792423 (lib. bdg.) | ISBN 9781680794106 (ebook) | 9781680794991 (Read-to-me ebook)
Subjects: LCSH: Cousteau, Jacques, 1910-1997--Juvenile literature. | Oceanographers--France--Biography--Juvenile literature.
Classification: DDC 551.46/092 [B]--dc23
LC record available at http://lccn.loc.gov/2016941516

Table of Contents

Introduction

Jacques Cousteau was an **oceanographer**.

He was also an inventor.
He made films about **marine life**.
He worked to protect the ocean.

Early Life

Jacques was born on June 11, 1910. He lived in France. He was often sick.

But he loved to swim.
Jacques also liked machines.
He especially liked movie cameras.

Leader

Cousteau studied the ocean.
He helped invent the Aqua-Lung.

It helped divers
move and breathe underwater.

He invented a camera.
It took pictures underwater.

He made underwater houses.
People called aquanauts
lived in them.

Cousteau explored the ocean.
His boat was the *Calypso*.

He made documentaries.
They showed marine life.

He also had a TV show.
It showed plants and animals.
He explained how people
were harming them.

Legacy

His TV show was famous. The films won many awards. They made people want to protect the oceans.

Cousteau started
a **society**. It teaches
people about the oceans.

It also protects marine life.
Cousteau died on
June 25, 1997.

Jacques Cousteau

Born: June 11, 1910

Birthplace: Saint-André-de-Cubzac, France

Wives: Simone Melchior (died); Francine Triplet

Known For: Cousteau made documentaries about ocean life. His inventions also helped people explore the oceans.

Died: June 25, 1997

Key 📅 Dates

1910: Jacques-Yves Cousteau is born on June 11.

1943: Cousteau and Emile Gagnan invent the Aqua-Lung.

1956: Cousteau's film *The Silent World* wins an award.

1968: *The Undersea World of Jacques Cousteau* airs on TV.

1974: Cousteau founds the Cousteau Society. It protects marine life.

1997: Cousteau dies on June 25.

Glossary

documentary - a movie or television show about real people and events.

marine - having to do with the ocean.

oceanographer - a scientist who studies the ocean and the plants and animals that live in it.

society - a group for people who share the same interests or activities.

Booklinks

For more information
on **Jacques Cousteau**, please visit
booklinks.abdopublishing.com

Z∞m In on Biographies!

Learn even more with the Abdo Zoom
Biographies database. Check out
abdozoom.com for more information.

Index